LISTEN TO YOUR HEART

A Guide to Living Life

On Purpose

Diane Ingram

Listen to Your Heart: A Guide to Living Life on Purpose by Diane Ingram

CreateSpace Publishing

www.createspace.com

First Printing May 2008

Unassigned quotations are by Diane Ingram.

Edition ISBNs

Soft cover   978-1-43820-903-6

Printed in the United States of America

Book Design and Photographs by Ron Ingram

Cover Design by Ron & Diane Ingram

This book is dedicated to

My three loves~
Ron, Ryan, Tyler

Who bring my purpose to life
everyday

Contents

Acknowledgements

Thank you to my husband, Ron, for twenty plus years of loving me and supporting the many projects I involve myself in, as well as supplying the beautiful photos that bring this book to life—thank you.

Thank you to my sons, Ryan and Tyler, for making me laugh, bringing me love, always reminding me how much I have to learn and to keep life light.

Thank you to my dear friend, Denise Dreany, for her many hours of precise and thoughtful editing, and for believing in my ability to write this book even when I was having serious doubts.

Thank you to my best bud, Debbie O'Brien for her lifelong friendship and generosity of time to review this book and offer insightful comments.

Thank you to my friend and mentor, Teri-E Belf, for her generous foreword and for her dynamic Success Unlimited Network®, LLC coaching program which has given form to who I am and what I have to give to the world.

Thank you to my parents for their love and for raising me with good values, particularly the "stick-to-it" one.

Acknowledgements

Thank you to Chris Farrell for the song-writing partnership that gives form to my creativity and spiritual practice.

Thank you to all of my clients whose adventures have taught me so much.

Thank you to all of those around me who had faith that this book was worth birthing into the world.

And finally, thank you to all who have inspired and educated me with their quest for understanding what it means to be human.

Foreword

A book with chapter titles such as *Sweet Dreams, Do You Believe in Magic?, Me and My Shadow, and What a Wonderful World* promises to be intriguing, inspirational and motivating. And this book is just that.

This book can be described as a compilation of all the wondrous personal discovery, self-help, and spiritual insights that have been the themes of so many books over the past 30 years—and all in one pithy book. Packed with a plethora of heart and purposeful messages, Diane has woven one easy-to-read fabric for us.

You can expect to explore the relationship between mind and heart, the connection between your lovable self and unlovable self-perceptions, the alignment of language and feelings, and your internal and external realities. Delving into this book is likely to raise your eyebrows (mind) and your vibration (heart), as the author states "Your mind is here to serve your heart, to take the actions that your heart deems worthy and desirous."

I wondered what more could be written about purpose having consciously been a student and teacher of purposeful living for over 20 years. As I began reading I recognized that my mind had been in charge of that initial thought, not my heart. Interestingly, I became very aware of my feelings while reading this book, and, existentially and viscerally, tuned into my heart while I reflected on the wisdom so clearly put forth. Sitting in an 1873 Victorian B&B feeling the radiating fire warmth, listening to my husband playing a real antique piano, peripherally seeing the pink, purple and turquoise splashes of color in this painted lady, I found myself transported into the very state Diane describes—awareness in the moment, an open heart, fulfilled and experiencing the joy of manifestation. Was it the book or the magical setting? I read the book again when I returned home and found my answer. It was the book.

Perhaps all this book is about is the *experience* of reading it or perhaps it is *all* about the experience. I encountered a paradox between my mission to write this foreword (using my mind) and my heightened awareness of my feeling sensations (beyond the words). Was it really a paradox? Pay attention to what you feel as you read this book. Unzip your curiosity for what your experience might be.

A painting is viewed through the eye of the beholder, whereas the artist who conceived it may have had a different experience in conceiving it. This book is about *your* experience as you read it. What do you choose to behold? You are holding in your hands an opportunity to explore how you see, feel and hear your heart as your beacon. You just might see something from a different perspective, or hear something you have heard before in a new rhythm, or feel inspired to do things differently, or feel motivated to make another choice. The possibilities are delicious when your mind serves your heart.

Speaking about artists, this book embraces a special treat, and worthy of a book in and of itself. Diane shares her artistic gift for headlining life's philosophy into heart-felt song lyrics as a melodious way to introduce themes and lessons.

The focus is not just about my experience or your experience. The author invites us to think beyond individual purpose -- to collective purpose as expansive as the context of our legacy to planet Earth. Read what might be possible beyond us when we listen to our hearts.

At some point one wonders, is this all too good to be true? For those who like to read about real-life experiences and how these pearls of wisdom have been applied, this book offers 'story time' scenarios sprinkled throughout providing evidence that it might be too good *and* it also might be true.

This is not the type of book you read and put on your bookshelf to attract dust. Keep this book by your bedside or on your office desk. Read it to your sweetie, your child, your friend, and your colleague. Keep one copy in your car to glance at when you are stuck in traffic. Take along a copy to read while you wait in a doctor's office, or are on-line to exchange something or . . .? Open it to any of the 30+ pearls of wisdom, observe, hear and sense how your awareness shifts to your heart. Allow your heart to be your guide to purposefully shine forth in our magical universe.

Teri-E Belf, M.A., C.A.G.S., M.C.C.

Introduction

Listen To Your Heart

Live the Moment

In the blinking of an eye
Life can quickly pass you by
Live the moment where you are
The past and future are too far from here

We pass each other on the street
Stop to chat or never meet
Move on quickly to what's next
Missing the moment,
Missing the moment.

We have a common ground all the same
Love and joy, sorrow and pain
Different scenarios to bring these feelings on
Experience the moment,
Experience the moment.

I extend myself to you
Heart and mind, and soul, too
That's the gift I have to give
The presence of the moment,
The presence of the moment.

The purpose of this book is to inspire and motivate you, the reader, to take action and make the changes necessary to live the life you desire in the deepest part of your being--and to start living it *now*.

As a life coach, people come to me wanting to make changes in their lives, to expand into their full, best selves. However, along with this wish is often an opposite wish: to put off for another day the work of focusing, changing habits and being consistent with changes. But life is lived now.

Life needs to be lived to its fullest in the moment we have, which is now. The more present we are to the moment that is now, the more empowered we find ourselves to make choices based on what *is* rather than what *was*, or what is yet to be. The present moment is where our power lives. How much of the energy of now are you allowing to flow through you? Or are you using some unimportant situation or circumstance to distract you and block it?

Are you the driver in your life, or the passenger? Who is at the wheel? Is it the long internalized voices of your past, perhaps your parents or your tenth grade teacher who told you that you would never make it to medical school? Is it your spouse or well-meaning friends who say fulfillment and satisfaction is for rich people? Is it society who says anyone who wants to be an artist is doomed to starve?

Listening to and following what your heart has to say makes you the driver. It gives you a clear map to follow that leads you to your best self. Our inner wisdom, intuition, speaks through our hearts in the form of desires, wishes and dreams. This inner wisdom is always with us. When we take the time to stop and listen, we are urged to take steps towards manifesting who we truly are and what we truly desire. The journey is revealed, step-by-step, for us to follow.

The headlights of a car only shine about four hundred feet in front of a car. That is all the driver needs to see at any one time in order to know where they are going. You can drive 3,000 miles across the county with only four hundred feet of light showing you the way.

It's the same with following your heart. You will be guided with the information you need to take the next few steps. Trust that as you stay open and receptive the rest will come and lead you where you want to go.

This book is a culmination of many years of learning from those who share my passion and fascination with personal discovery and development. At the beginning of each chapter you will find lyrics which I have set to music. This is another way in which I access the language of my heart.

I offer what I have come to know to be true for myself and from my experience with others who have taken action to embrace the life they desire to live. My hope is that you will find inspiration and value in my words, and that these words will smooth the way for you as you travel down the transformational road of self-discovery. Enjoy the journey!

It's My Life

Listen To Your Heart

Who Am I and What Am I Doing Here?

She wakes in the morning and jumps out of bed
Shakes all the night dreams right out of her head
Runs to the bathroom and looks in the mirror
Wonders, "Who am I and what am I doing here?"

She climbs in her clothes and runs out the door
Steps in her car and puts pedal to floor
She's spinning her wheels and she wants it clear
The answer to" What am I doing here?"

Time to take a moment, sort out her thoughts,
Touch deep inside for who she is
And who she is not

Her family & friends have her well pegged
To be what they need her to be, but instead,
Her self is transforming as it appears
By asking, "Who am I and what am I doing here?"

She sees that she needs to refine
Beliefs of the hand in her life of divine
She promises herself that this is the year
To explore, "Who am I and what am I doing
here?"

© 2005 Lyrics by Diane Ingram/Music by Chris Farrell

Awareness

Being present to the moment that is *now* heightens our awareness, not only of ourselves, but of our place in the universe. Being present to the moment allows us to tap into a deep inner stillness that connects us to deeper consciousness.

A way to remain present is to practice what Eckhart Tolle calls "embodiment". Focus your awareness on the aliveness in your body. Sense into what's going on inside. This brings you right into the present moment in an instant.

We are all expressions of consciousness in form. Our journey is to expand our consciousness through awareness, and to bring the light of that consciousness into the world. When we are aware of our individual purpose, we are fully expressing the uniqueness of that consciousness. As we spend our time and energy on the things that reflect our purpose, we bring aliveness, passion, and meaning to our lives. When we connect with our purpose, we invite inspiration in, give ourselves permission to express our true selves, and feel the joy flowing through that expression in our lives.

When we realize our purpose, we bring to the world something that hasn't ever existed before in this particular way. It is not for us to determine if what we have to offer is good enough or worthy enough. Our life work is to pay attention to, stay aware of, and be open to what excites and engages us, and then focus on being, doing, and creating those things that excite and engage us. In doing this, we become vehicles for expanded consciousness in the world.

We are energetic beings vibrating along with everything in the universe. We are pure energetic consciousness in form, whose source is the intelligence of the universe. The more we are aware of this, the more we can recognize ourselves in everything. The more we consciously participate in the transformation of our lives from ordinary to extraordinary, the more we can participate in the transformation of the world from a sometimes chaotic and discordant one, to one in which all people experience their fullness of being and their magnificence. Imagine what that would be like!

Shifting Perspective

Often we walk around feeling so small and insignificant, as if our lives didn't matter. We try to convince ourselves that we are worthy to have the things in our life that we want, to do the things our heart calls us to do, but get stuck in the question— "Am I good enough?"

This question reflects a cultural paradigm of lack, scarcity, and separateness. Our capitalist culture thrives on and perpetuates the belief that by spending our money on clothes, gadgets, toys, bigger and better houses, powerful cars and exotic vacations, we will find happiness, fulfillment and enhanced identity. Without these things, we are not good enough, don't measure up, aren't successful. In trying to find ourselves in *things*, we instead end up losing ourselves. We need to bring awareness to this paradigm, look deeper within ourselves and see where our true happiness is to be found.

A better question would be -- "What do I want to feel and experience in this moment now, as well as the years I have on the planet, for myself and the highest good of the universe? How do I want to design my life so that I can experience this level of deep satisfaction and fulfillment most of, if not all the time?"

If you are stumped by these questions, you are not alone. The desires and passion that we come into the world with have been lost, or shoved to the corner of our consciousness because of familial and cultural prohibitions on experiencing joy, magic, and wonder. The puritanical beliefs that much of our culture's mindset is based on are that life is hard, one must go for the money and get the goodies—no matter what that means as far as life style or impact on the planet—in order to survive and be secure.

The problem with this paradigm is that many of us are "living lives of quiet desperation", as Henry David Thoreau so powerfully stated. We are living with a numbing emptiness and a feeling that our lives are meaningless. We attempt to fill the emptiness by buying ourselves things, filling our closets, garages, kitchens, burying ourselves in stuff; numbing ourselves with work, busyness, doing for others; filling our stomachs with food we don't need, our blood levels with alcohol, our social life with people we don't care about. But it is an emptiness that can never be filled in this way. It is a lifestyle that is destroying our planet from over-consumption and unconsciousness.

We have been convinced that this is the non-selfish way to live—doing always for others, doing the proper thing, sacrificing our desires, while unconsciously filling the empty void inside with stuff and letting the chaos take over our lives. Selfish is defined as going for what we really want. We actually have it backwards. . .

Turn It Around

When we are fulfilled from within, our energy is directed toward doing the things that bring us a deep level of fulfillment. This, in turn, enhances our lives and the lives of those around us. When we are feeling deeply satisfied, fulfilled and joyful, we are filled with abundance within and experience life as abundant; we are feeling vibrantly alive. From this vantage point, over-consumption seems excessive and wasteful. We re-prioritize our time and values, and choose to consume just what we need and no more.

Life takes on a shimmering quality, and we experience beauty and grace in ourselves, and the world around us. When we vibrate at this level, our relationships improve exponentially. We have happiness to give to others. They experience our satisfaction, our joy and peace within, and are inspired to emulate that satisfaction, joy and peace for themselves.

It is the opposite of selfish, because when we are living on purpose, we are giving our best gifts to the world. We are being expansive and generous, coming from this place of satisfaction and fulfillment.

The world needs these gifts, now more than ever, in order to transform into a fulfilled, healthy planet. When we are generous with ourselves and others it fills our hearts so completely that love spills out of us spontaneously. It's a win-win for all.

Being part the world, we have an effect on it, positively or negatively. By transforming ourselves and raising our level of personal happiness, we can affect the world positively and provide a benefit for all of life. Now is the time for us to own our responsibility and consciously choose our affect on the world.

Power of Purpose

Our soul has a deep desire to express itself in ways that channel joy. Our job is to discover what that is and to activate it in our life.

By choosing our life's work because it will bring us toys and money, live out the family dream, or one that is the "in" career to pursue at the time, we design our lives from the outside in. This can result in feelings of meaninglessness because it is not connected to who we are at our core.

When we choose to design our lives from the inside out, expressing ourselves on purpose, we design our lives through the lens of what will make us happy and bring fulfillment to who we are, which by definition is meaningful and satisfying.

Experiencing who we are and what we do as one, being congruent, we feel alive and that our life has meaning. There will still be times when life is challenging, when there may be a rock or log to navigate around, but we will feel like the river is flowing. We will feel we are in the right place, even if it is not exactly where we ultimately want to be; we recognize it as a step on the path to a self-actualized, meaningful life.

Discovering Who We Are

Discovering our life purpose focuses our attention on the essence of who we are—our being. So how do we discover our heart's calling, our purpose on this earth, our gift to give?

I spent many years thinking if I only knew what my purpose was, I would know what to do with my life. Somehow if I searched hard enough, it would be revealed to me. I have come to realize that my purpose is found inside me, not handed down from some source in the sky; it is perceived by the qualities that are important to me—what I feel the passion and desire to do, to be, to create.

I completed the life purpose process (see *Facilitating Life Purpose* by Teri-E Belf under Resources), by looking at the times in my life when I felt deeply fulfilled and satisfied, and clarifying the specific well-being qualities that allowed me to feel deep satisfaction and fulfillment. From those qualities I created my purpose statement:

My life purpose is to transform
my heart and the heart of the world,
through grace and beauty,
to find fulfillment, magic and surprise.

Now that I am clear about what my purpose is, the gift I uniquely bring into this world for manifestation, I feel a sense of belonging, validation and acknowledgement for who I am. I feel an enthusiasm about my contribution, what I alone bring to the party that wouldn't be there unless I attended. And now I have moved from the question of "What is my purpose?" to "How do I want to design my life so that I am fully expressing and living it each day?" And that is a wonderful, creative place to live from.

You, too, have a purpose that represents what you bring to the party—the unique role you play in the universe. And, once you discover what that unique role is, it becomes a touchstone, a reference point that will guide you toward decisions and choices that will leave you feeling wonderfully fulfilled and satisfied. It offers you the possibility of leaving the world a much richer place because of your gift, your unique contribution that you can manifest and give to yourself and the world.

It's the essence that you came into the world with and will carry with you throughout your life. Ideally it will be expressed through your work, allowing full manifestation of your gift, although it can also be expressed in many other areas of your life as well: in your family life and primary relationship, community, volunteer and social life, spiritual life, how you express yourself creatively, in your health and self care.

What is it that you dreamed of long ago? To be a writer, teacher, singer, dancer, chef? To make a difference in the lives of children or disabled or struggling people? To invent or create ways to ecologically support the planet? What qualities of well-being would the realization of that dream bring to your life? What events in your life, big or small, left you with deep satisfaction? A success you experienced in childhood? Being acknowledged as a leader at work? Helping someone who needed to be taken care of? What success in other people's lives do you envy? Whose life would you like to have for your own? These are all clues as to what is on purpose for you.

A gardenia seed can only grow into a gardenia flower—and what an intoxicating, scented, beautiful flower it is. If it tries to be a tulip or an orchid, it is an impossible task that would lead to frustration, loss of energy and failure. It is the same with us. When we try to become something we are not, we experience frustration, loss of self-esteem and vitality. Being clear about who we are and what we need, helps us create strong, healthy roots with colorful, elegant blossoms.

Your Vastness

Live in the vastness of who you are. As fellow SUN coach, Joan King talks about in her book *Cellular Wisdom*, the goal of the every cell that makes up our physical form is to thrive. Cells vibrate with positive, life-giving energy. As with cells, our life is a process of unfolding and activating unseen potential.

We are so much more than our circumstances, the families we were born into, the jobs we have, the country in which we live. We have been conditioned by these things in our lives and now subconsciously conform to certain ideas and viewpoints, but we are so much more than the limited views these conditions give us.

We are the vastness of consciousness manifested in the here and now. We are unique expressions of universal intelligence. As we awaken to our vastness and make choices in the daily creation of our lives from that awareness, we create a life that reflects the size of our beings – a full, magnificent life. We begin to realize that who we are does matter, the choices we make and what we do with our lives matters, we are worthy and we have the power to affect the world in amazing ways for the good of all living things.

Opportunities and Possibilities

Life Purpose calls to us from the deepest recesses of our being—we just need to take the time and be still to hear the call. When we are living our purpose, we experience a profound sense of flow—being in the right place at the right time, using our gifts. When we are participating in activities that stretch us toward our future selves, we experience this flow as being in "the zone". As Daniel Goleman says in his best selling book, *Emotional Intelligence,* "Flow is a state of self-forgetfulness, the opposite of rumination and worry: instead of being lost in nervous preoccupation, people in flow are so absorbed in the task at hand, that they lose all self-consciousness . . . they are unconcerned with how they are doing, with thoughts of success or failure—the sheer pleasure of the act itself is what motivates them."

As we create life out of who we are, it becomes a rich adventure of opportunities and possibilities. We become open to this adventure, experiencing the helping hand of the universe through synchronistic events. By using our purpose as a beacon, a light shining on our path, it guides us to make choices that align most with who we are. At that point, the whole world opens up.

The spiritual teacher Joseph Campbell said, "When you follow your bliss, doors will open where you would not have thought there would be doors, and where there wouldn't be doors for anyone else." Keep your eyes open for those opening doors—they are a sign that you are on the right path.

As the world rapidly evolves and changes at a very fast pace, there are exciting opportunities that will come into existence that we haven't yet imagined. By focusing on the qualities that are important to us, we can follow the thread, being open to new opportunities as they become available.

When we live a life on purpose, of purpose, opportunities and events seem to come out of nowhere and support us in the fulfillment of that purpose. Synchronicity, that often appears magical in its perfection and timing, starts happening in our lives. We attract energetically what we are clear we want to create. Vibrating at the same frequency as that which we desire, like a magnet, it is attracted to and drawn to us.

Story Time

Amy was halfway through college, but had no idea what she wanted to do when she graduated. She came from a family, like many, who never asked the big questions; who were so busy living day-to-day to meet what seemed like the incessant needs of living, that there was no time for such visionary exploration.

So she took a semester off, only to find herself more lost and confused. By the time she had contacted me for coaching, she had worked herself into a dark hole of pessimism and depression. Life was starting to resemble a treadmill of chores, never adding up to anything worth getting excited about, with no apparent larger purpose.

After doing the life purpose process, she became clear about what qualities are important to her and bring her satisfaction and fulfillment: creativity, beauty, ideas, inspiration, accomplishment, independence; and what the essence is that she brings to the world. With her purpose as her map and coaching support to create a plan of action, she has confidently stepped into forgotten dream: designing and arranging interiors for the perfect balance of beauty and usefulness. She finally feels in the right place, making a success out of something she loves.

What do you feel called to do with your years on earth? How do you want to be in this world for the precious time you have left to live? What fuels you, brings magic to your life?

"Without purpose we often climb to the top of the mountain, only to realize it's the wrong mountain".

Marcia Weider

"I've come to believe that each of us has a personal calling that's as unique as a fingerprint. And the best way to succeed is to discover what you love and then find a way to offer it to others in the form of service, working hard, and also allowing the energy of the universe to lead you."

Oprah Winfrey

Sweet Dreams Are Made of This

Listen To Your Heart

My Heart's Desire

My heart's like a boat out on the sea
sailing for lands that set me free
fear aside, I ask my deepest self
what do I hunger for my life to be?

My mind's like a canvas waiting paint
landscapes defined by my beliefs
tuning in to what my heart craves
my mind supports what I can see

I dream the dream of a thousand dreamers
yearning for my heart's desire
to be the one I came here to be
fulfills my heart's desire

Our lives are like flowers bursting forth
opening up with brilliant hue
as we bring to light our gifts to share
the world becomes so much richer, too

What Is It

When I was five years old, I started formal ballet instruction that lead to a deep love of dance; any kind of movement actually. I also loved to sing and was good at it. I was acknowledged for my voice with solos both at church and at school assemblies. I came to know myself through these creative expressions and when I was actively doing these things, my spirit would soar.

But these expressions were viewed in my hard working family as hobbies, something to be relegated to the perimeters of my life. I was advised to pursue a much more practical livelihood. When I went off to college, instead of studying music and dance, I received a Bachelors Degree in Child Development, with a minor in

Psychology. The study of psychology fed my curiosity about human beings and what makes them tick; what allows some to lead profoundly satisfying lives, while others are forever mired in their mental issues and baggage.

I loved children from my years of babysitting and helping at the church nursery, but it wasn't the same as what I experienced when I sang and danced. The yearnings of my heart nagged at me for years until I decided to listen and honor them.

I taught myself some basics of music theory and practice, and started writing songs. In 2000, I produced my own CD of original music. I now collaborate with a local musician, writing songs of personal healing and transformation. We are currently in the process of producing a CD of these original songs. And as a life coach and motivational speaker, I get to have deep conversations about what matters most to people and support them in designing their life to reflect these things. Now, everything has shifted and life has assumed its magical glow again.

What excites us, ignites our passion, doesn't go away, no matter how much we may try to dampen it down, or how much it gets dampened down by others. It remains there in our hearts, calling to us in the still, small voice that lives deep within our being.

In your wildest dreams who do you want to be? What is the dream you have dreamed for your life? What did you long to do back before you were told it was impossible?

For some of us, these questions were answered when we were young, with confidence and self-assurance, backed by family support and encouragement. And then there are others who had the answer and lost it: buried under a pile of opinions: family members, teachers, others in our lives who told us that we were better at doing something else rather than what we longed to do; creating confusion and raising doubts about our own dream ever coming true.

But we each had and still have a dream for our lives. We may not want to hear it, thinking it is too late to realize or too difficult to take action towards, but we each have one. What is yours?

Get In Touch

This question can not be answered accurately by your mind. Your mind is here to be of service to your heart, to take the actions that your heart deems worthy and desirous. You must be willing to enter your heart and dialogue with it. There you will find your wisdom—the answers to all of your questions, if you take the time and make the space to be still and listen.

Begin to get in touch with what your heart desires. Get still, quiet your mind, and go to the deepest part of your being. Listen closely and don't discount what you hear. It is your higher wisdom speaking to you that must be heard and honored. As you start to act on this wisdom, you begin to trust it more and more. Allow yourself to feel what it would be like to finally have your dream come true. By allowing yourself to fully feel the excitement, passion and joy of manifesting your dream, you fuel your vision, which attracts corresponding energy from the universe and further actualizes your desires. By focusing your thoughts and feelings on what you want, you clarify your vision and invite the universe to help create it.

As life on the outside starts becoming congruent with who you are on the inside, it feels satisfying, engaging and full of the qualities of well being that are important to you. If what you hear in your heart speaks to you in the language of growth, expansion and love, you can trust that it is truth for you.

As trust in yourself grows and you develop a relationship with your inner wisdom, you discover the true source of your power and can see the spark of divinity within you. Allow yourself to experience the calm, safe, secure feeling of knowing that you hold within your heart the answers to your deepest questions. Find peace and solace in that knowledge. Make room for that inner wisdom to be heard, honored and followed. Living tuned in and guided by to this inner wisdom means life circumstances will come and go, while you stand centered and grounded in the truth of who you are.

Well-Being Qualities

What are the qualities of well-being that are important to you? Underneath everything we do, are well-being qualities that come with doing those activities. What is it you enjoy doing? What does that activity bring to your life in terms of your state of being? Do you experience fun being with friends? Accomplishment when you challenge yourself, finish a piece of work? Peace and connection when you walk in nature?

When we are clear what well-being qualities are important to us, we can choose those things in life that bring us a larger and more intense experience of the qualities that we want to be experiencing. Harmony, peace, fun, freedom, confidence, living in the moment, what is it for you?

When we design our lives around living our desires and dreams, we are able to live in a larger, more vibrant place. As we take steps in the direction of our dreams and see it starting to be realized, life takes on a shimmering, magical quality. We begin to have faith in our ability to manifest what we want, to shape and transform our lives in the way we choose. We feel more and more empowered to create a life beyond our richest imagination.

In order to begin this journey, we need to let go of the known and step into the territory of the unknown. It requires openness and trust that we will find fulfillment in living our truth. The dream changes and evolves in expression and form over time, but the essence remains the same—a deep reflection of who we are.

Just starting the process of creating the life of our dreams brings energy, inspiration, satisfaction and joy—the joy of a journey down a road that feeds our soul and speaks to our deeper selves.

Story Time

Twenty-year-old Connor's desire was to express himself creatively in the world. He went to college for a brief period of time, but felt stifled by all of the academic demands placed on him, that seemed to have no connection to his creativity.

His creativity took many shapes—designing t-shirts, writing and playing music, drawing mechanical objects. When he was being creative, time stopped and his heart soared. He was anxious to be out of college and so he could put these ideas into form.

By getting the support he needed to trust his intuitive voice, he became clear that, at this point in time, he wanted to explore taking his creativity into the world. And so he has designed a plan to make that happen.

He is now creating t-shirts with environmental awareness designs and selling them online—this supports him financially so that he can make recordings of his music. He recently joined a touring band, singing their original songs to audiences around the country. He is living his bliss.

Who knows what's down the road for Connor. For now, he is just following what his heart indicates are the next steps—the ones that fill him with enthusiasm and enjoyment—and seeing where that takes him. Life is satisfying, and it is just the beginning of a rich adventure for him.

So what gets you excited, enthused, and energized? What do you find yourself wanting to give to others?

"I have learned that if one advances confidently in the direction of their dreams, and endeavors to live the life they have imagined, they will meet with a success unexpected in common hours."

Henry David Thoreau

"Your vision will become clear only when you look into your heart. Who looks outside dreams, who looks inside awakens."

Carl Jung

Do You Believe in Magic?

Listen To Your Heart

Into the Unknown

The view from my window is stunning
frozen earth covered in white
bare trees touching each other
support for birds taking flight

Into the blue they (I, we) soar
destination not clear from below
part of me goes with them
into the unknown

What's beyond my window
there on the other side
destiny holds what tomorrow brings
I go along for the ride

Let go to the pull of the forces
let go and take a chance
a challenge worth accepting
the universal dance.

©2000 Lyrics and Music by Diane Ingram

Other's Opinions

People in our lives sometimes like to tell us who we are: "You are not good at math; you ought to be going for that teaching job; acting is hard work. . ." These messages can be helpful in pointing the way or shining a light on our path, giving us direction. However, oftentimes, they are the projections of the people around us— expressing their own fears and/or dreams unrealized, having very little to do with who *we* really are. Trying to separate these projections from who we are can be difficult.

When we hear these messages over and over again, at the very least, they are confusing; at most they can send us down a path of frustration and destroy our sense of self understanding and awareness. Consistent thoughts create a groove in our brain that becomes a belief. We can unwittingly form subconscious beliefs around these opinions from others that greatly limit and distort our concept of who we are, what our limitations and possibilities are, how the world works—the list goes on and on.

Beliefs and Choices

From the set of beliefs that we have unconsciously assumed, we make choices, and get results that confirm the beliefs on which we based our choices. It is a never ending loop, until we decide to raise our awareness, choose new beliefs that support our growth, and discard the rest.

> ➤ Our Beliefs

> ➤ Inform Our Choices

> ➤ Which Create Results

> ➤ That Confirm Our Beliefs

When we are able to raise our awareness, to make conscious the subconscious beliefs that run our lives, they often begin to drop away. We can choose whether these beliefs support expansion, growth and realization of a wonderful life, or leave us stuck in a box of limitations, frustration and resignation. When we move beyond our habitual beliefs, we can take the lid off the box, look around and see things from a whole new perspective, a wider range of possibility. We can then choose to step out of the box, which brings to our life a whole new array of choices with which to create our life.

Years ago I did a fire walk with Tony Robbins in New York City. It was the early eighties and he facilitated self-empowerment seminars that ended with an eight-foot walk across hot coals. It was a life transforming experience. I saw that with focus, concentration and new beliefs, I could do anything. The walk illustrated for me that the only thing limiting the possibilities in my life are the self-imposed limits in my own mind. The walk facilitated a powerful shift in realization that ANYTHING IS POSSIBLE, if I believe it to be so. It was indisputable —I walked across the coals and didn't burn my feet.

From this experience, I went on to run two marathons, complete a triathlon, do many creative endeavors, write and produce a CD of my original music and become an entrepreneur. I also went on to produce several plays, serve as president of my running club and to hold other leadership positions. The fire walk gave me an enhanced sense of courage and possibility which did serious damage to my previous beliefs of limitation and doubt.

We have the freedom to choose what we want for ourselves in each moment. We are making choices all the time, every moment of our lives. Often the small choices have the largest impact. How do I start my day—in a spirit of gratitude and appreciation or grumpiness and resistance? What do I feed my body that will give me the fuel for all I want to accomplish, create and be today— healthy, nutritious food or junk food?

Even when it seems as though there is no choice, if we look close enough, we'll see there is always a choice—even if it's just the choice of attitude. Victor Frankl in *Man's Search for Meaning* says, "Forces beyond your control can take away everything you possess except one thing, your freedom to choose how you will respond to the situation. You cannot always control what happens to you in life, but you can always control what you will feel and do about what happens to you."

When we remain aware of this truth, we are empowered to create our lives in the manner in which we desire. We can be in the most confining of circumstances and choose whether to stay in the situation, mentally rise above it or remove ourselves from it.

When we start to pay attention to choice, we realize that, day to day, we completely create our lives by the choices we make. What freedom and power that awareness brings! We can transform our lives by the choices we make, based on our purpose, values and inner guidance, each and every moment on this earth.

Values

What are the values beneath the choices you make? When we are involved in projects, involved with people, and in places consistent with our values, we experience feelings of energy, congruence and enthusiasm. These activities reflect qualities that are important to the way we want to express ourselves in the world. The blending of purpose, gifts and values allows us to experience our wholeness.

When we are not living a life consistent with our values, we can experience ourselves as inauthentic and frustrated. We can feel trapped in lives that don't hold much meaning for us and we don't know why. As we develop a deeper understanding of what our values are, we can choose to act in ways that express those values in our daily lives.

We find clues to our values by looking at how we spend our time, where we spend our money and energy, and who are friends are. If we are not living the values that we say are important to us, we need to make changes so that our lives in the world are in line with our deeper values. Congruence between who we are on the inside with how we are living our life out in the world, allows us to connect with our authenticity and experience peace in our lives.

The Religion Paradigm

We live in a culture that holds many religious values – of good and bad, right and wrong, and the belief that we are all judged and controlled by some authority outside of ourselves.

As we come to realize that the choices we make cause a reaction and spiritually affect ourselves and our world, the thoughts behind what we choose take on a larger context. It is not about whether some abstract authority figure will deem us worthy of entering heaven by our attempts at doing acts of goodness; but that we find the goodness that is already within us, and that we recognize that the choices we make here on earth affect others. When we take responsibility for and ownership of that, everything shifts. We realize that it is within our power to be self-determining, to create our lives.

Clearing Beliefs

What gets in the way of you creating your wildest dream? When you hear "Anything is possible, you can have it all", what thoughts come up for you? Any negative thoughts and beliefs that come into your mind when you start approaching your dream are clues as to what is getting in the way of you having your dream. As you become more aware of the negative conditioning you have assumed, the beliefs that sub-consciously run your life, you are able to re-choose.

Allow yourself to feel these beliefs fully. These particular beliefs may have served some purpose for you earlier in life—to protect you or keep you safe. Do they hold a purpose or message for you that resonates with who you are today?

See if you can separate them into specific, individual beliefs. Ask yourself if you now still believe that this particular belief is true. What would happen if you stopped believing it? Are you using fear of starting something as a tool to help avoid failure? Do you think your belief of not being good enough is what makes you stay on good behavior? Or is your belief of not being good enough keeping you safe in your comfort zone, free from stepping into the unknown and trying something new?

As we discover these old beliefs lying around in the dark corners of our mind, we find that they are unconsciously running our lives or at least tripping us up. By doing a little investigating, shining a light in those corners, we become free to release them. We recognize and acknowledge that they may have served a purpose once in our life, but are now in the way of our self realization. We can then release the beliefs that no longer serve us into the universe. In doing so, we lighten our load of old baggage and free ourselves to move forward into our dreams.

What would be a new belief, a replacement of the old belief that supports us in expansion and growth? How about affirming: "As I listen to the inner urges of my heart, I am safe and supported to live an abundant, fulfilling life"? We can visualize with feeling, affirm and repeat these new supportive beliefs as they become part of who we are now. The feeling connection is important because it activates the energy around the affirmation and anchors it in our heart.

Our beliefs about ourselves are based on our history and our past conditioning. To be more current and accurate with who we are now and who we are becoming, we must spend time each day reinforcing, with visualization and affirmations, the beliefs that support us in becoming our full, realized selves.

When the old beliefs are cleared, our energy is able to move in the direction of our desires, not scattered every which way, fueling old beliefs. By getting out of our own way—removing the "shoulds", the rules, the old voices that have held us back, we can begin to create our future. Listening to and following our heart opens us up to creating what we desire, what's fun for us, what allows joy to enter our lives and take hold.

Carolyn Myss in her book, *Anatomy of the Spirit*, talks about imagining we have 100 parts of energy each day. If half or more of them are tied up in defeating beliefs, we feel drained and depleted, and are left with very little energy for what we want to create. It is imperative for us to clear these beliefs lurking in the shadows so that we can have all our energy available to create our day, to live our life to the fullest. This provides the freedom to grow into the vast, magnificent beings that we are.

Story Time

Kim came to me so overwhelmed by the opinions and voices of others, about who she was and what she should do with her life, that she couldn't hear her own voice. She had convinced herself that it was far less painful to fulfill the family's dream of her becoming a lawyer, even though her heart was not in it, then to excavate her own dream out from under the family pressure.

As she was about to graduate from college, feeling very uninspired about continuing on to law school, she started to experience health issues for the first time—low energy, repeating viral infections, depression.

After getting clear on the values and qualities important to her, finding her strength, and realizing she has the power to make her own choices, she created a vision for her life and how she wanted it to unfold—and she's well on the way to making it happen. She envisioned a career of making an impact in the lives of disadvantaged children and began exploring careers where that impact could be best actualized. Fortunately, while in college, she did follow her heart a bit and take classes that will assist her in this area of expertise.

This clarity of vision also gave her the strength to be honest with her family and to speak powerfully to them from her heart. They now enthusiastically support her in her journey of self discovery, exploring what she wants to do in life.

What paths have you gone down that are not your own? What dreams have you fulfilled that belong to others? What pressures have you succumbed to that have taken you away from your original desire?

"Until you make the unconscious conscious, it will drive your life and you will call it fate."
Carl Jung

To accomplish great things, we must not only act, but also dream, not only plan, but also believe."
Anatole France

Me and My Shadow

Listen To Your Heart

The Gift of Grace

Waking from our slumber, looking for the light
Spinning round in circles, caught up in the night
Open up and see it, move the veil away
It's sitting right before us, the brilliance of the day

As we set our hearts on fire, with the glow that
shines inside
Burning through, brilliant light

We find it's all right here
Within our hands
The gift of grace

Wake up to the wonder, bursting with surprise
Elements of magic, right before our eyes
All the love in heaven, is right here in our heart
Open up and feel it, let it light a spark

©2006 Lyrics by Diane Ingram/Music by Chris Farrell

The One in the Mirror

The psychiatrist Carl Jung created the theory of the "shadow". His theory is that when we are young, we learn from other people in our lives that parts of our selves are unacceptable— certain emotions are not welcome: sadness, anger, even too much happiness or enthusiasm; certain ideas or talents that threaten the status quo; certain behaviors that are considered inappropriate or wrong.

In order to be accepted and loved, we push these parts of ourselves into the dark corners of our psyche and they become our shadow. Enormous amounts of energy are needed to control and suppress those parts of ourselves that we believe are unacceptable—energy that is unavailable for us to use in other ways.

If these aspects of ourselves are left unacknowledged or denied, they often cause negative, unconscious behaviors to emerge at unexpected times and in unconscious ways, affecting our lives adversely.

Often, these behaviors will look like they are coming from people in the external world. We project our shadows and beliefs onto the world, which then reflects them back to us.

Everything that we see and feel in our world is a reflection of the state of our own consciousness. We may feel scared, unworthy, insecure and doubtful of ever being able to fulfill a larger purpose in our life. The reflection that we get from others, gives us the opportunity to become aware of these shadow beliefs and the state of our own consciousness. Whatever is showing up in our lives is an indication of the point of growth for us at that particular time.

We actually attract people and situations into our life that hold the possibility of illuminating our blind spots and provide us with an opportunity to heal those areas. The stronger the negative response we feel to a person or situation, the more urgent it is to cast some light in that corner to reveal what's really going on.

Whenever we are judging or criticizing someone or something, we are resisting an aspect of ourselves that we have not yet accepted. Jung says "everything that irritates us about others can lead us to a better understanding of ourselves".

Instead of using criticism and judgment to separate ourselves from other people or situations, we can choose to be the observer and rediscover parts of ourselves that we have disowned. We can choose to not take things personally, but to observe what there is for us to learn. This then requires us to take what we have learned and make changes in ourselves, gently and compassionately.

When we become aware of those aspects of ourselves that we have hidden and shine a light on them, we free up vital parts of ourselves wanting to be recognized and expressed. We also free up tremendous reservoirs of energy and wisdom that we can use to propel ourselves towards new possibilities and opportunities. We must be willing and able to hold ourselves in all of our complexity, both darkness and light, with love and compassion.

With acceptance, forgiveness and empathy, we can find true peace in our wholeness.

Acceptance

Accepting that the present moment holds all the wisdom we need—the lessons, awareness and beauty of the moment—brings an incredible peace to our lives. We no longer need to wrestle control, trying to change what is and make it go our way. This frees up so much energy! Then, instead of being powered by the negativity from rejecting what *is*, we are powered by life, living in alignment with the present moment. We can then relax and trust in the path of acceptance, paving the way for our enlightened choices about the future.

As we accept our whole selves and learn who we are, compassion and love for ourselves and those qualities that we possess is able to breathe and grow. And when we clear one area of our lives, major shifts often start spontaneously occurring to help clear up other areas of our lives.

When we are willing to forgive ourselves, we become more able to forgive others—forgiveness, being about letting go of the longing for a better past, deactivating the memory of the pain by not rehashing it constantly, and freeing energy to envision a different future.

When we feel love for ourselves, we are more able to love others. We can only offer others what we are able to actively give ourselves.

Take the time to listen to your heart and get to know yourself better. Let it speak to you from this deeper level of wisdom, which will make you more available to give the world the gifts that it so needs you to give.

Story Time

Jennifer's childhood had been one of feeling unwanted, unappreciated and unloved. She carried these wounds with her into the present and lived life as a victim in every encounter. She was so busy blaming others—family, friends, co-workers, whomever she interacted with—for all the shortcomings in her life, no one stayed in her life for very long. She wanted so much to connect with others, to have more friends and even a life partner, but people just pulled away from all the negativity. She was incredibly lonely, even making *that* other people's fault, not able to see her role in it all.

With compassionate directness from her
coach, she saw that she had the power to choose
differently and take responsibility for her life. This
was a painful, albeit enlightening, awakening. No
longer playing victim to circumstances, she was
able to accept her life for what it was and change
the parts that needed changing. She found that
through loving and appreciating herself, she no
longer resented others for not stepping in to heal
her wounds. She had the power to heal herself.

This made her much more appealing to be
around and helped her to cultivate a social network
of caring friends, colleagues and a potential
partner. She felt empowered to get involved and
make a difference in her community. And most
importantly, she was at peace with who she was.

"One does not become enlightened by imagining figures of light, but by making the darkness conscious"

Carl Jung

"Without darkness, nothing comes to birth, as without light, nothing comes to fruit."

May Sarton

Imagine

Listen To Your Heart

Listen to the Silence

Stepping outside of our usual lives
of coming and going and doing
we can step inside to the center of being
Taking a moment to find the solace within

Listen to the silence
It speaks volumes
Listen and be still

Listen to the silence
It speaks to who you are
Listen, listen to the silence

Taking the time to go to our core
we find rich and fertile ground
we can turn inside and touch the soul
Take a moment to find our essence within

And when we hear the soul's song
like the silence of a sunrise
we align ourselves
with a world of wisdom and light

© 2006 Lyrics by Diane Ingram/Music by Chris Farrell

What You Focus on is What You Get

It is estimated that we have 60 thousand thoughts a day, give or take a few thousand . . . So what are you spending your time thinking about?

Our mind is programmed by the input it received when we were young, as well as what we repetitively input currently. We program our minds with movies, news, other people's opinions, thoughts, ideas and images from our imaginations, whatever we allow in. Our mind is like a search engine—searching and finding examples in the world that reflect our beliefs, the way things are for us. We create our life from our thoughts and our beliefs, whatever we spend our time thinking about and focusing our attention on. By changing our thoughts, we literally change the quality of our lives.

The first step to changing our thoughts is to focus on that which makes us feel good and brings us joy. Some of us have been trained to see the glass as half empty instead of half full. We obsess about what's not working, which brings us more of what we are focusing on—the half empty glass, or what's not working.

By appreciating, acknowledging and being grateful for what is right about ourselves and about our lives, we can build on that appreciation, acknowledgement and gratitude which, like a magnet, attracts more of it into our lives.

As we begin paying attention to and becoming more aware of our thoughts, it is

important not to lapse into judgment or despair
when we realize our thoughts are often habitual,
repetitive and negative.

It is important to be compassionate with
ourselves, knowing that this is a process that takes
time. As we raise our awareness and gently,
gradually, create new habits of mind that help us
refocus on what we want to be thinking, feeling,
doing, we begin to create the life we have long
dreamed of living.

In a *Daily Om* (www.dailyom.com) reading
it says, "We harness the power of the mind when
we choose supportive, healing thoughts. All we
need to do is remember to tend the field of our
mind with the attentive and loving hand of a master
gardener tending her flower beds, culling out the
weeds so that the blossoms may come to fruition."

Tend your garden well; it completely colors your experience of life.

Deep Listening/Intuition

When we take time to tune-in and listen deeply to ourselves, we receive valuable guidance. Intuition, our inner guidance, is operating all the time. If we choose to listen to it, we will connect with the wisdom of our higher self, making choices that are aligned with our purpose.

This intuition can come to us as a mental message or image, or through symbols and synchronicities. The more we become aware of the meaning of these messages and symbols in our lives, the more we increase our communication with our deeper selves: our intuitive power.

Intuition also speaks to us through our feelings. As we tap in and feel the power and wisdom they hold, we experience that power. The challenge is to be able to distinguish between intuitive guidance and the projection of our fears. Sensing into our feelings, if we experience grace and flow, that is intuitive guidance. If we experience upset and resistance, that is an expression of our fears.

Feelings

We are, by nature, feeling beings. They pass through us constantly. They are not to be judged as good or bad, right or wrong, but simply to be experienced. If we give them the space to exist, we will experience them and then they will move on, leaving behind a wealth of information about ourselves and our world. If we deny or ignore them, we block our power. Whether we want to act on these feelings or not, is our choice. But the primary purpose of our feelings is to energize us, raise our awareness and enhance our experience as human beings.

Arnold M. Patent has a wonderful exercise to help us reconnect with and feel the pure power that resides in our feelings, as described in his book, *"You Can Have It All"*:

- ❖ Feel the feeling, free of any thoughts you have about it. Feel the energy, the power, in the feeling.

- ❖ Feel love for the feeling just the way it is. Feel love for the power in the feeling.

- ❖ Feel love for yourself feeling the feeling and feeling the power in the feeling.

Creation

By discovering and valuing our dreams, thoughts and feelings, our vision starts to take shape, clarifying who we are and what we want to create with our lives. We make a deeper connection to what is really important to us. By listening to our heart and what it yearns for, we raise our awareness about our desires and then the potential creative energy can begin to emerge and take shape.

We are creating all the time. As our heart opens and we recognize who we are and what we want, we become a clearer channel for the creative energy of the universe. The more love and positive feelings we experience, the more we can shape the creative energy for the good of all.

Story Time

Jim's life was successful on the outside, dry and brittle on the inside. He had some creative yearnings, some ideas about what would bring spice to his life, but felt stuck in the confines of his already packed world as husband, father of three young children, president of his web design company, and town councilman. Just getting through the week was a major accomplishment. But he wanted more—more meaning, a real connection with himself.

Listening closer to what his inner wisdom was telling him, he reprioritized and chose to spend more time doing what got him excited and engaged: more quality time with his family; picking up the guitar regularly and writing songs, which also helped him to access and process his feelings; going for daily runs to set the tone for his day. These small changes elevated the quality of his life—simple, small changes caused major transformation in his being. He now checks in with himself regularly to stay clear and focused on what's important to him as his creations evolve.

Life is about creating. Are you satisfied with what you have created thus far? How are you spending your energy—in frustration and depletion, or happiness and fulfillment? How can you bring more playfulness and light into your creation?

"The intuitive mind is a sacred gift and the rational mind is a faithful servant. We have created a society that honors the servant and has forgotten the gift."

Albert Einstein

"When you are inspired, dormant forces, faculties and talents become alive, and you discover yourself to be a greater person by far than you ever dreamed yourself to be:"

Patanjali

Come Together

Listen To Your Heart

Connected To All That Is

Sitting by the lake at the dawning of the day
The sun casts an arc of brilliant gold
Its reflection on the water
Radiates into my heart and mind and soul
And I feel connected to all that is

Sitting by the lake as it awakens full of life
Two eyes look at me looking at them
We recognize in our gazing
Kindred selves in elemental reverence
And I feel connected to all that is

A great peace, washes over me
I receive, the love in nature's grace
As I melt into her embrace

Sitting by the lake as the gentle breezes blow
A tree bows into the wet beneath
Dancing leaves move to and fro as
Spirit comes alive in sacred revelry
And I feel connected to all that is

Good Vibrations

Our being is made up of energetic vibrations. Everything in the universe is vibrating energy, and we are always interacting with this energy. When we are living a life on purpose, we tap into a higher level of vibration that is more aligned with the intelligence of the universe. When we align with this higher vibration, we experience more expansion, beauty and peace. When we are blocking and resisting this energy, we experience discomfort and frustration in our lives.

In a state of expansion, beauty and peacefulness, we open to the infinite intelligence of the universe, which is contained in all energy. It is always available to us. When our minds are calm and our hearts are open, we can hear and feel this intelligence, as well as see our own essence reflected in it.

When we consciously choose to surround ourselves with a support network of people who accept our purposeful essence as real, we quickly learn the power of mutual support in bringing our purpose to fruition, to lead a more fulfilling life, and to have more fun. Our essential purpose is always present. Beneath the doubts and fears resides our real self, which is pure love. Anytime we look for this love in ourselves and in others, we find the essence of who we truly are.

The higher our vibration, the more we positively contribute to the vibration of the world. The more we are radiating light and love, the more we are bringing light and love to the world. It is always our choice—what we will give to others, what level of vibration we will share with the world.

The universe is a supportive one. There is a natural flow of abundance. There is an infinite supply of energy available to us, to replace any that we have given out. The more we ask for support and are open for help from unexpected places, the more amazing synchronicities begin to happen. Many times we can achieve our goals effortlessly by letting the universe handle the details. We can create the vision, begin to take action, but also let go a bit and surrender to our new life emerging.

Accepting the perfection of the universe and how it works encourages us to trust our universe and everything and everyone in it, beginning with ourselves. The result is a free flow of energy around and through us and a feeling of aliveness. It allows our lives to unfold in effortless and magnificent ways.

We Are All One

We are all connected at the deepest levels of our beings, and we are influenced by the energetic vibrations of everyone around us, whether we are aware of it or not. As our lives become more peaceful and aligned with purpose and fulfillment, our vibration level rises and that energy is picked up by others as comforting and supportive. This encourages others to reach for higher vibration levels within themselves, even though they may not be aware that they are doing so.

Our role is dual—to expand beyond our own belief systems and to support others to expand beyond theirs, which plays itself out as an improved quality of life for all. The combining of all of our vibrations determines our overall quality of life and the higher the vibration, the higher the level of consciousness of everyone and everything on the planet.

As Lynn McTaggart talks about in her book, *The Field*, we are all points of white light. We are all connected. We swim in a sea of light, the zero point field, essence to essence, which is the true state of our being. Seeing yourself as perfect just the way you are, expresses the truth of who we all are, allows our level of vibration to rise and allows us to experience our oneness with all other beings. As we focus on our oneness rather than on our separateness, we become vehicles of transformation of consciousness.

Story Time

As my client, Philip became more aware of his personal power, through clearing some negative beliefs that were stopping him and taking small action steps out of his comfort zone, he experimented with his ability to affect the energy of various circumstances in his life. Due to some recent layoffs and a downsizing in his company, the morale at his office was low.

He decided to experiment with consciously effecting that situation. He envisioned light emanating from every cell of his body and touching others, igniting their cells to light up. He sent positive, affirmative energy as well as verbal acknowledgement to every one he came in contact with in the office.

He felt he was able to effect and elevate the level of interaction to one of support and excitement, which then spread throughout the space, having a positive, inspiring effect on all the other people he encountered. He discovered, clearly and undeniably, that how he is being has an immediate and direct impact on all those he comes in contact with. His goal is to remain conscious of this as he goes through his life. And by the way, business started picking up. . .

"We cannot live for ourselves alone. Our lives are connected by a thousand invisible threads, and along these sympathetic fibers, our actions run as causes and return to us as results."

Herman Melville

"The life I touch for good or ill will touch another life, and that in turn will touch another, until who knows where the trembling stops or in what far place my touch with be felt."

Frederick Buechner

"And as we let our light shine, we unconsciously give other people the permission to do the same. As we are liberated from our fear, our presence automatically liberates others."

Marianne Williamson

What a Wonderful World

Listen To Your Heart

Like A Pebble Dropped in a Pond

Like a pebble dropped in a pond
that ripples throughout the whole
each one of us touches everyone else
with who we are, with what we say, with what we
do

In our day to day lives
we can choose our attitude.
How will we be with each other?
Will we judge, or let be?
Will we give empathy?
Will we choose to spread kindness to all
and be a star, a guiding light in the night?

In our day to day lives
we can choose our way to act.
How will we care for creation?
Will we use and pollute,
or honor and renew?
Will we choose to spread reverence on earth,
and be a star, a guiding light in the night?

©2006 Lyrics by Diane Ingram/Music by Chris Farrell

Legacy

Legacy represents everything we are in this lifetime and what we leave behind when our lives end. We leave a legacy no matter what—some of us leave behind gifts that represent the best of who we truly are, others not so. When we participate fully in the world from the place of our strengths, passions, doing what we do best, we leave an inspiring foundation for others to build upon.

Do you want your legacy to extend beyond your life, ripple out and touch others in meaningful ways? A legacy of contribution emerges from a life lived consistent with purpose, contributing positively to the planet. We create a field of consciousness as we pursue our purpose individually and collectively. By bringing our best gifts to the world, we can literally expand and shift the consciousness of the planet.

Imagine that you are at the end of your life looking back—what have you accomplished that is meaningful and fulfilling, not just for you, but for mankind?

Elisabeth Kubler-Ross, pioneer of work with death and dying, said that those at the end of their life most often asked variations of these three questions:

- Did I give and receive love?

- Did I become all I can be?

- Did I leave the planet a little better?

In order to become fully realized human beings, we need to discover our authentic reason for living—a reason that is bigger than we are. We need to answer the question, "What is the primary manner in which I seek to make a difference in the world?" Eckhart Tolle says in *A New Earth* that a bigger question than "What is my purpose?" is "What does the world expect from me?" I think it is both and that both questions can be resolved with the same answer.

Our Gifts

One of the gifts that we come into this world with, given to us by an abundant and loving universe, is the unique talents that we are each blessed with. These are not just the talents that are easy to recognize like a talent for drawing or an affinity for numbers, these include talents like comforting a child or diffusing a tense situation. Recognizing where our talents lie and being willing to express them is the key to releasing and channeling our deepest joy.

Our ability to successfully express our unique talents and purpose is determined by how much love we feel for ourselves. When we love ourselves, we not only acknowledge our talents and purpose, we delight in practicing and expressing them. As we uncover our talents and gain confidence and comfort in expressing them more freely and fully, we get better and better at it. Our talents, used in the service of our purpose, combine to create a powerful synergy of creation.

In touch with our purpose, every conversation counts, every encounter is an opportunity to touch or serve another, and every moment can be precious and meaningful.

Service

Each day we can choose how we will give our gifts to the world. Through giving of ourselves, we find our true self. One of the biggest evolutionary steps in our self actualization is a shift from looking at how life is fulfilling our expectations, to realizing that life expects something from us. When that shift occurs, magic starts to happen. In service we feel our life expand and enrich, as we experience being a part of something larger than our finite lives.

Our purpose is only fully realized when it is brought to the world. Once we become clear about what we have to offer and its value, it becomes our responsibility to take it out into the world. We begin to witness how our purpose supports the greater well-being of the whole, as well as creating a larger context in which to live our lives. And we get to experience the ultimate joy of contributing to the beauty, power and perfection of our magnificent universe.

Story Time

John was a successful businessman who felt that his life was meaningless. It seemed like he trudged off to work each day with no apparent larger vision. He wanted his life to be about something more than making money and indulging himself with more things.

We started the coaching program by clarifying his life purpose and then creating visions of what each area of life would be like if he were living life wildly on purpose. We then brainstormed about practical steps to take that would help him reach his visions and live the life he had imagined.

He had married, but never had children. When he became clear about what his purpose is, what makes him happy and brings meaning to his life, he decided to manifest his purpose through volunteering as a Big Brother, mentoring a boy without a father.

This was such a rich experience for John that he went on to participate in a community teen program, sharing his business skills with young future entrepreneurs. Making a difference in the lives of others beyond himself brought incredible meaning and satisfaction to his life.

How do you want to feel you have made a difference, affected the world? What is your work to do on this earth?

"When you are able to shift your central focus to how you serve others, you will be in a position to know true miracles in your progress toward prosperity."

John Donovan

"Personal transformation can and does have global effects. As we go, so goes the world, for the world is us. The revolution that will save the world is ultimately a personal one."

Marianne Williamson

Conclusion

Discovering and fulfilling our purpose requires focus, discipline, consistent action, listening and staying in touch with what our heart has to say to us. We need to get to know who we truly are—not who others are telling us to be—and live in that place fully.

We need to be willing to make mistakes, and then go back again and again to our heart's wisdom for guidance. We need to be gentle and compassionate with ourselves as we walk this path of self actualization. And as we do these things, life opens up to a state of joy never realized before.

There is beauty and wonder all around us. Bathe in it, look for it—don't let these magical experiences slip by you. These experiences are ours for the taking. That is what we are here to do—to live life to the fullest by seizing opportunities and possibilities that speak to us; to love with all our heart and drink in with our senses the glory of nature; to participate in the joyous experience of being in a physical body on this beautiful planet earth; and to tap into our rich, inner world by listening to our hearts.

"Twenty years from now you will be more disappointed by the things that you didn't do than by the ones you did do. So throw off the bowlines, sail away from the safe harbor, and catch the trade winds in your sail. Explore, dream, discover."

Mark Twain

The Jewel in the Heart Meditation

Find yourself in a comfortable sitting or lying position. Close your eyes. Take a nice, deep breath through your nose and let it out through your mouth with a sigh. Again, inhale through your nose and let it out through your mouth with a sigh. Do this several times as you allow yourself to come more and more into the present moment and relax deeper and deeper.

Scan your body for any tension, starting at the top of your head and slowly working down to the soles of your feet. Notice wherever your muscles are holding on—breathe into those areas and release.

As you let go, allow your body and breath to peacefully settle in. Know that you are in a safe place, supported by the surface your body is resting on, and it is safe to let go and relax.

Gently and slowly bring your attention to your heart. Allow your breath to gently massage and soothe your heart.

Envision a jewel in the center of your heart—a glistening, sparkling jewel with many facets. What is the shape of this jewel? Notice the color. Allow it to be whatever it is.

There is light both emanating from and reflecting off of this jewel—a bright light. What are the colors of this light?

Allow this light to bathe your whole body in a sense of well-being. From top to bottom you are filled with loving light that illuminates every cell of your body.

Allow this light to go beyond the bounds of your body and fill the room. Feel the fullness of the light.

Send this healing, loving heart light to anyone in particular or to everyone on the planet. You can even send this light to the far reaches of the universe. Feel the expansion of the light.

Now, slowly and gently, bring your awareness back to the source of this light—the jewel in your heart.

Is there a message this jewel holds for you? Ask and receive this message. Be open to whatever form it may take—a thought or feeling, images or words. Be flexible with the timing of the message—you may receive it now or it may come later.

Know that the jewel in your heart holds your inner wisdom. Trust that this jewel can act as an anchor for you, a point from which to ground and center your being.

You can contact this jewel in your heart whenever you want—in meditation, driving in your car, interacting with the world—use it's wisdom for guidance and direction as you go through life. This is your intuitive guidance. This is listening to your heart.

When you are ready, return your attention to your body. Feel yourself in your body, Feel the surface your body is resting on. Take a deep breath and let it out. Open your eyes.

Audio MP3 file of this meditation available for a free

download at

www.dianeingram.com

Joy

Joy, it lives inside of us
Sparkling bright
Precious jewel
Facets of every shape
Reflecting light

Joy, untouched by circumstance
Go with the flow
Accepting self
Contentment in our core
When we come home

Joy, maker of pure delight
Essence of who we are
Joy, grateful to be alive
Glistening in our hearts

©2007 Lyrics by Diane Ingram/Music by Chris Farrell

About the Author

Diane Ingram is a Motivational Speaker and a Certified Life Coach who received her certification through Success Unlimited Network® and is credentialed by the International Coaching Federation. She is also a lyricist and author in the field of self-development.

She brings these experiences, as well as being an athlete and parent, to her work to access the best in people and to help them find purpose and meaning in their lives. She lives in the Hudson Valley region of New York with her husband and two sons.

Please visit <u>www.dianeingram.com</u>

> ➢ **To purchase more copies of this book**
> ➢ **To book a speaking engagement and view speaking video**
> ➢ **To schedule a free coaching session**
> ➢ **To sign up for a free newsletter**
> ➢ **To download audio meditation file**

Resources & Suggested Reading

Teri-E Belf, *Facilitating Life Purpose*, Malibu, CA, Purposeful Press, 2005.

Daniel Goleman, *Emotional Intelligence,* New York, New York, Bantam Dell/Random House, Inc. 1995

Joan C. King, Ph.D., *Cellular Wisdom*, Berkeley, CA, Celestial Arts, 2004

Ervin Laszlo, *Science and the Akashic Field: An Integral Theory of Everything,* Rochester, VT, Inner Traditions 2004

Richard J. Leider, *The Power of Purpose: Creating Meaning in Your Life and Work*, San Francisco, CA, Berret-Koehler Publishers, Inc., 1997

Bruce Lipton, *The Biology of Belief,* Santa Rosa, CA, Mountain of Love/Elite Books, 2005

Lynn McTaggart, *The Field: The Quest for the Secret Force of the Universe*, New York, New York, HarperCollins Publisher, 2002

Carolyn Myss, *Anatomy of the Spirit: the Seven Stages of Power and Healing*, New York, New York, Three Rivers Press/Crown Publishing Group, 1996

Arnold M. Patent, *You Can Have It All: A Simple Guide to a Joyful and Abundant Life*, New York, New York, Pocket Books/Simon & Schuster Inc. 1995

Cheryl Peppers & Alan Briskin, *Bringing Your Soul to Work: An Everyday Practice*, San Francisco, CA, Berret-Koehler Publishers, Inc. 2000

Eckhart Tolle, *A New Earth: Awakening to Your Life's Purpose*, New York, New York, Plume/Penguin Group, 2006

Eckhart Tolle, *Stillness Speaks*, Vancouver, Canada, Namaste Publishing, 2003

Joe Vitale, *The Attractor Factor*, Hoboken, NJ, John Wiley & Sons, Inc., 2005

1549861

Made in the USA